SAVOURING VERSES

A JAMAICAN CHILDHOOD (RE)COLLECTION

JUDITH SHAW

Savouring Verses: A Jamaican Childhood (Re) Collection
Copyright © 2025 by Judith Shaw

First Edition 2025

ISBN:
Hardcover: 978-1-998245-51-2
Paperback: 978-1-998245-50-5

Cover and book design by Kabrena L. Robinson
Published by Eva-Michelle & Family Publishing
www.evamichelleandfamily.com

*"..... food has a culture. It has a history.
It has a story. It has relationships."*

-Winona LaDuke

Contents

APPETIZERS OF MEMORY

Light bites of nostalgia to whet the appetite

MAIN COURSE: A FULL PLATE OF CULTURE

Rich savoury pieces seasoned with history, tradition, and ancestry.

SIDES & SOUL FOOD

The small things that carry big flavour

DESSERT: SWEET ENDINGS

Sweet reflections, joy, play and cultural cravings to close the feast.

Forward

*J*udith Shaw is authentic to the bone. A dub poet, author, and storyteller, she brings rhythm, heart, and spirit into every line she writes. Her words dance with the pulse of the island—vibrant, unapologetic, and full of life. Her stories are rooted deep in culture and carry the sweet, rich flavour of home.

Savouring Verses: A Jamaican Childhood (Re)Collection is just that—a full-on sensory experience. With every verse, you're drawn into warm childhood memories, the sound of laughter on the verandah, and the scent of something delicious drifting from the kitchen. It's a walk down memory lane — one delicious bite at a time.

Judith serves us a cultural feast, blending poetry and prose the way our elders did—with love, laughter, and care. These aren't just poems—they're moments. They're the smell of hardo bread fresh from the bakery, the joy of mango season, the sound of your grandmother humming while she cooks.

As you read, you'll smile, maybe even tear up a little, and definitely feel hungry. Most of all, you'll feel the love—for family, for community, and for Jamaica.

Savour each verse. Let it fill you up and wrap around you like a warm pot of Saturday soup.

Kesha Christie
TEDx Speaker
Award-winning Storyteller

Acknowledgement

*B*efore anything else, mi haffi give thanks.
To the ones who poured into me, stood by me, reminded me of who I am, and cheered me on from near and far—this book could not exist without you.

Thanks to my husband Gary for his unconditional love, tremendous support, and tolerance.

To my beloved sons, Rashidi and Nathaniel—open up your heart's creative chamber and allow the artist in you to flow.

Thanks to my mother, Halet, for teaching me to always sit and walk with my back straight.

Thanks to mi fren, Shushanna Harris, for all your encouraging words.

Thank you, Kesha Christie, for giving me a space on Talkin' Tales year after year to share my art.

Thank you, Greg Frankson, for the Black Lit Durham stage.

Thank you, d'bi.young anitafrika, for advising me to prevent imposter syndrome from killing my artistry.

Big up mi Jamaican culcha!

A yuh mek dis possible.

"Mi love yuh like a fresh vegetable."

From di bottom of mi heart,

mi tank yuh.

Preface

*S*avouring Verses: A Jamaican Childhood Re(Collection) emerged from a place of love for mi Jamaican culture, language, and childhood experiences—especially where food was concerned.

Mi smile with mi belly full up with joy when mi remember the days walking barefoot on the street to buy bulla from the bakery on South Camp Road for my grandmodda to sell and for the household to eat. Mi mout' a run wata—lawd, bulla nice when it warm. Oh, and those days—those after-school days—when I purchased a bag of stewed June plum and eat them with enjoyment, licking the caramelized juice off my fingers and elbow. What a sweet, delightful recollection.

My eyes glittering with satisfaction, remembering buying a bag of sky juice from the sky juice man. And I still can hear him chanting, as if I was standing on Cross Road this very moment: "Sky juice, sky juice—come and get yuh bag of sky juice!" Wow —my childhood days were fulfilling, sucking on a bag of suck-suck. Words cannot express the immense nostalgia I feel within. So what better way to share some of my childhood joy with others but through the artistry of poetry?

Savouring Verses: A Jamaican Childhood Re(Collection) is a book of poems that are light, fun, and a bit cheeky. You will also get a taste of my childhood place.

APPETIZERS OF MEMORY

Light bites of nostalgia to whet the appetite

Nostalgia

Nostalgia satisfies my soul.
It feeds me,
it feeds me well,
with sweet, sweet memories.
The taste of yesterdays
still remains crisp
I am nurtured,
and full from
wistful food.

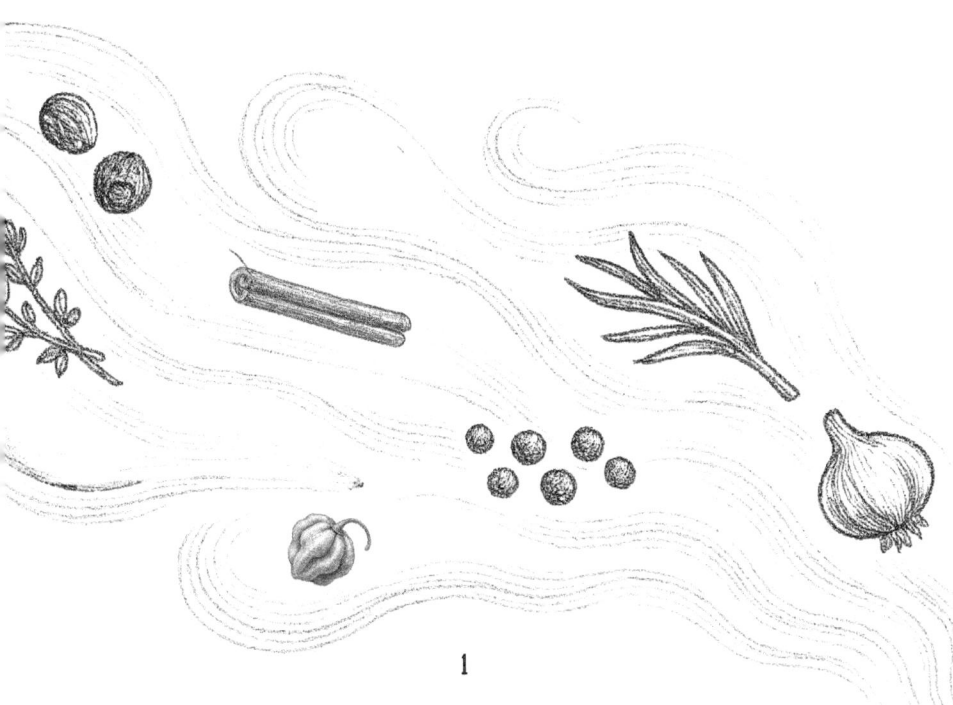

Reminisce 'Bout Old Times

Yesterdays come and gone,
but they still live on, on.

Come, let me and yuh sit down fi awhile
and reminisce 'bout old times.

Remember how we used to
sit under the Julie mango tree—
you sip pon some hot cerasee,
and me sip pon some hot peppermint bush tea,
with excelsior crackers a soak and a float.

And we used to smile with our hearts open up wide,
a take in the sweet, sweet sunshine.

Come, let us sit down and lap we fracktail,
and labrish 'bout the old days.

Remember how some of those days
use to make us hold we belly and laugh,
full up of joy–

and some of those days really made us
halla out–
"Have mercy, good Lawd!"
We had to beg Him to give us the strength
to keep the pillow and plead for Him to take the case.

Dem days did surely put us through the test, mi dear.

Don't get me wrong–
me nah try to pick up spill milk,
but nothing wrong wit' walking down memory lane
and picking out some pieces
of yesterdays.

Me believe, seh
a so stories live on and on,
so me and you can recall dem today,

and hope for the next generation
to retell dem in futurity days.

Ting

Give mi the drink dem call Ting—
green bottle sizzling with grapefruit zest,
sparkling like Jamaican sunshine—
nothing but the best.

Refreshing like the cool breeze
off Blue Mountain peak,
it's a zing-zing when you take a sip.

When you take a sip,
you taste a bit of paradise,
sizzling on top of your lips,
straight down to
the tip of your toes.

Suck Suck

Childhood memories–
refreshing, like
suck-suck.
A frozen coolant clutched to our
lips and our tongue,
a pacifier for that heated sun,
and hydration during our games and fun.

Bring me back—
reminiscent, sweet like suga,
with a squeeze of tangy lime
and a splash of Kool-Aid colour.

Please, bag it and freeze it,
so that I will always remember.

The Sky Juice Man

It was at the corner of Cross Road–
busy intersection—
the Sky Juice Man's song
blasted over
people's chatters and laughters,
their hustling and bustling
and the traffic's screeching and beeping.

The Sky Juice Man held his tunes
and sang out loud with determination.

"Sky juice!
Sky juice!
Come over here
and get yuh bag of sky juice
and stay cool.

Lady in the red
and lady in the blue,
Taxi man,
and school yout'
one for you too!"

The Sky Juice Man's lyrics
rippled through the atmosphere
like music from a dancehall selecta's speaker box

and hit the patrons' earwaves.
His rhythm pulled them closer to his stall
and each one dipped and danced their hands
in pockets, purses, and wallets.

Sky Juice Man smiled brighter
than the afternoon sunshine.

He bagged two scoops of shaved ice
and pumped selected flavoured syrup–
all the white of the ice
evenly coloured.

The patrons took their refreshing delight.
And irie away with a cooling smile.

Sky Juice Man blasted his song
in the atmosphere
once again.

"Sky juice!
Sky juice!
Come over here
and get yuh bag of sky juice
and stay cool.

7

Holy is the Hardo-Bread

Holy is the hardo-bread.
Blessed are the souls who
partake in it when it is warm.

Break into it–
eat it plain, or with margin, or with butta,
without any restraint.
With each bite, you feel like
you are in heavenly paradise.

Praise di Lawd–it's Friday!
The day the baker's bell starts ringing,
a calling for all the hardo-bread patrons
to come marching in,

prepped for the weekend feast.

Saturday–
hardo-bread with callaloo, fish fried or steamed,
or with any of your favourite delicacies.

Sunday comes and you beg and pray
that a piece of hardo-bread is left
to grace your plate
before the sun is set

Monday, Tuesday, Wednesday, Thursday—
not even crumbs spared
for the ants to take to their nest.

Anticipation rises
as Friday approaches,
to hear the baker's bell start ringing—

'Cause holy is the hardo-bread.

Manish Wata

I remember you
at nine-nights,
when the community gathered with the bereaved
to celebrate life—
and you anointed them
with your flavourful roasted goat head
and diced-up green bananas in well-seasoned wata.
And everybody's cup runneth over—
Manish wata,
 you truly satisfied their soul.
And they remembered the deceased without grief and sorrow.
And all night they sang—
they sang joyfully.
And all night, the dominions played like musical instruments
on the table tops.
And all who played, played joyfully.
It was a night to always remember.

The Blood Purger

You are the one they call Bittah—
green-leafed bittah-ness,
old-time country people
bring-to-town healer.
They say you got the healing powah.
Bush tea from country,
you are the natural remedy—
the blood cleanser,
the blood purger.
Cerasee, yuh run through my memory.

MAIN COURSE:
A FULL PLATE OF CULTURE

Rich savoury pieces seasoned with history,
tradition, and ancestry.

Come Let Us Travel Back

Come let us travel back
to Port Royal,
where the ferry boat docked,
and children dived and swam like dolphins.

And where you savoured the taste
of escovitch fish and bammy.
Bammy—what a tasty delight.
Cassava lingered pon yuh tongue
after every bite.

Onion, scotch bonnet pepper, carrots,
and allspice,
sautéed in vinegar, or maybe with lime,
decorated over the fresh fried fish—
flavour colourful and pleasing to the palate,
as it is to the eyes.

And then cool this succulent heat down
with a glass of ice-cold fruit punch,
or with a cold, chilled bottle of Ting.

Licked yuh lips and rubbed yuh bellyful,
when yuh sit down and dine pon
escovitch fish and bammy
by the ocean shoreline.

My Grandmother Was Music and a Dance

My grandmodda never teach me how to cook,
but lessons were learned as I listened to her
hum along to the rhythm of the bottle,
beating against the thyme and scallion.

And I watched her body move
with rhythmic motion while she crushed
fresh garlic with a spoon.

Yes, my grandmodda was music,
and she was a dance in her own kitchen.

She lit the gas stove with one stroke of a match.
I witnessed her wrist flash to the trombone notes of–
"Simmer down; can you hear what I say now",
I swear Don Drummond was near.

I watched her hands clutch the Dutch pots,
and sweet cymbal sounds echoed throughout.

I saw my grandmodda's whole body move like Jonkonnu
when she rolled her cornmeal flour dumplings–
round and tight, just how she liked.

When my grandmodda peeled the skin off the green bananas,
her fingers glided to the beat of–

"Come, mister, tally man, tally me banana."

Oh, it was a day.
It was a sweet, sweet, delicious day, O Belafonte,
when my grandmodda Wawa
was in her kitchen, cooking.

And when she stripped, washed, cut up, seasoned up,
and stewed down the callaloo,
I heard the sounds of–
"praise the Lord, oh my soul."

And I watched her dance the puukko dance,
her whole body moved in full control.

I watched my grandmodda rock steady
when she hoaxed out, grated, squeezed,
and milked the coconut,
tapping to the melodies of–
It was "unda the coconut tree."
Yes, Miss Lou, darlin'.

When my grandmodda washed her rice,
tambourine melodies vibrate from the palm of her hands
right down to her waistline.

Believe me when I tell you this–
when my grandmodda brown-stewed the chicken
and curried the goat,
she sang on key and danced
without missing a beat.

14

Johnny Di Dread Was a Good, Good Cook

Johnny Di Dread lived inna one tenement yard in Allman Town, pon Hitching Street. Him dreadlocks did long—right down to his belly. Him wasn't too dark skin, and him wasn't too light skin. His complexion was just nice and cool. **Johnny Di Dread** wasn't too tall and he wasn't too short. Him wasn't skinny, and him wasn't fat either. Johnny had an average height and an average weight size. Johnny did love fi smile, and him did look irie all di time. Him sold cook food fi tek care a him family. Him cooked from a board-up kitchen, right in front of a zinc-up gated yard pon Hitching Street.

Me a tell yuh—**Johnny Di Dread** created fi him own original style of patty. Him kneaded his dough with cornmeal, and him stuffed some with fresh callaloo, some with fresh ackee, and some with callaloo mixed with ackee—

then him fried dem. **Johnny Di Dread** was a vegetarian, so him cooked strictly ital food. Dem seh **Johnny Di Dread** complexion was so cool because him eat strictly ital vegetarian food. Him did eat only foods dat grow under di ground, food from deep inna di sea, and food from the trees above. No salt is added when him cook and when him eat. Him would steam him fresh fish inna fresh coconut milk, with fresh okra and fresh pumpkin. Johnny cooked the best fish and corn soup inna di whole town. Johnny was a good, good cook. Fi him food did taste sweet and nice—to me and to everybody else who buy it. Yes, fi real—**Johnny Di Dread** was a good, good cook. And him smiled and looked irie all di time.

Ital

Rice and Peas

If I may,
I will serve and share this tasty childhood joy with the world
and awaken everyone's palate;
and let each one relish in its delight.
Slowly, I will feed you one teaspoon at a time,
so this enjoyment may linger.
My one desire is to allow this pleasant taste to remain
constant on tongues—
for all to salivate every time
your thoughts reflect back to this moment—
this moment when I share and feed you
rice and peas.
And with each bite, you will savour the taste of the
 subtle sweetness of coconut,
with a tender burst of scotch bonnet pepper,
 garlic, scallion, thyme, and pimento.
And as you consume one of Jamaica's Sunday traditions,
your enjoyment will heighten
with unforgettable pleasure.

Curry Goat

If I to write about a certain cuisine
and all the celebrations it has been—
all the weddings,
all the birthday parties,
all the nine-nights,
and all the events fit for queens and kings...
I will also tell yuh
of the satisfying pleasure,
di delectable taste it brings.
And when curry goat cooked
authentically—
oh Lawd, have mercy,
it is mouthwatering.

Stew Peas

Mi can't recall how often my grandmodda
cooked stew peas.
In retrospect, I cannot remember her cooking it at all.
Was stew peas a meal for other homes?
Was it because of salted beef and pigtail,
submerged in the sweet, tasty coconut cream—
with kidney beans and fresh spices—
and just before the final
stretch of the stewing,
spinners dunked in?
Or was it because it took hours for the pot
to cease from bubbling and boiling,
and boiling and bubbling?
But how did I know this?
In which home did I learn it?

Dutty Gyal

remember dis: "Memories don't leave like people do."
So me always remember you,
with yuh tomato sauce pasty self,
and a throw stones like only sardines pack up inna can.
And when we check it out—
yuh a tin mackerel pack up inna can too.
So dutty gyal,
gwan with your fishy self.
My granny Wawa always tell mi seh,
"If you want to get rid of any **dutty gyal** fishiness—
just add piece a scotch bonnet peppa, thyme, scallion, and onion
inna a hot pot of cooking oil,
and **dutty gyal** will simmer down just right.
Remember to sprinkle likkle black pepper too,
mi child, and never forget, to squeeze likkle lime."
So dutty gyal, tin mackerel in tomato sauce,
my grandmodda gimme the right remedy
fi rustle you up at any time mi feel like
with dumpling and stemed rice.

Mackerel Rundown

Let's rundown mackerel—
salted mackerel.
And when yuh fetch it,
settle it down in some fresh coconut cream
and fresh seasonings.
Love it down with
 boil dumplings
and a couple finga
of boil green bananas.
And I know fi sure—mackerel rundown
will comfort yuh soul
on those days
when it is cloudy and grey.

Susumba

I could never forget
susumba—
dis backyard, roadside, riverbank, gully beans,
clustering berries, tiny and green.
Bitter to the tongue,
but sweet with cooked-up saltfish
and mackerel rundown.

Licked Dem Fingers 10 Times

Dem seh chicken back too bony—
dem called it poor people's food.
But when we run-a-boat
and cooked up chicken back with curry,
dem nyam and chew it up in a hurry,
licked dem fingers 10 times.
And we hear dem hum softly—
"Dis is a sweet, rich, flavourful food.
We must give tanks fi small mercies."

Bully Beef

And from Grace, we received it—
canned and keyed.
But memories unlocked the many times—
the many times we sandwiched it,
the uncountable times we cabbaged it,
the numerous times we paired it with rice,
the heap of times we piled it on top of green bananas,
yellow yams, or dumplings,
and the many times we nyam fried plantains with it.
And we always seasoned it—
scallion, thyme, and scotch bonnet it,
ensured the right amount of black pepper sprinkled pon it.
Garlic, onion, and tomato had to know it.
We understood it was not just a can of bully beef—
it was also our staple, affordable meal.
And as a culture, we took care and pride
in the preparation of tin corned beef.

It's Friday Night

"Party hunting and feeling right."
As I reflect on Johnny Kemp,
"Just Got Paid, It's Friday Night" video—
I saw the resemblance of the days on the island
when pay cheques were paid.
People nuh cook a dem yaad,
and everybody a food vendor hunting
on Friday night.
And the vendors were feeling nice,
because everybody was buying
what they were selling.
The feeling good inside
was reflecting on everyone's smiles.
The vibez was right.
Appetizing aromas engulfed the atmosphere.
It was a carnival of food—
jerk pork,
jerk chicken,
fried fish,
steam fish,
roast fish,
roast corn,
fish soup,
corn soup,
boiled carbs,
roast yam.

The selection was more and beyond
what our stomach could contain.
But the vibez—the vibez was nice,
and everybody was feeling festive inside.
Friday night was a night of full delights:
music,
chatter,
laughter,
happy people,
and good food everywhere in sight.

Grandma's Cooking

Have you ever felt like having a meal—
a meal that takes you back,
that takes you back
to a place of childhood peace?
Where the comfort of grandmother's love
was so real—
but as a child, you did not know
that it was grandmother's love
that made the meal so satisfyingly comforting.
But adulthood has led you down the path
of wisdom and understanding—
that yes, it has been love,
sweet, sweet love,
in all of Grandma's cooking.
'Cause no one else
can make that meal
as tasty and satisfying.

Ben Johnson's Day

Home was a place
where the mango tree and ackee tree
give something to eat, sometimes—
and where tenants exchange suga fi floua, sometimes.
And some days,
Grandma cooked only rice and butta fi dinna.
I wonder today—if on those days Grandma
cooked only rice and butta fi dinna—
were those the days of Ben Johnson's Day?
As I sit and wonder
on those childhood days,
I can truly answer:
they were filled with wondrous
fun, games, and play.

A 7-Day Menu

No matter the weather throughout that day,
Saturday was known as the soup day.
Sunday arrived—breakfast was hefty and nuff,
and at dinner time, rice and peas was a definite must.
And whatever left over, served fi Monday dinna.
And when Tuesday comes, anything goes fi suppa.
But back pon track on the next day because
white rice and stew peas a grace yuh Wednesday plate.
And if yuh couldn't find a nickel fi spare,
dawg nyam yuh suppa, because Thursday a Ben Johnson's day.
Thank God it's Friday—
not only because you just got paid,
but yuh can find a food vendor everywhere.
And each one of dem happy like a lark,
'cause nobody nuh cook a dem yaad.

Soup Day

Soup day was not just a regular day
in Jamaica, mi dear.
It was a tradition for the sake of the island's goodness.
Saturday was the chosen day to
clean house, wash clothes, and cook soup
before the daybreak.
And when the cleaning, and the washing, and the cooking
were all done,
we all rested well
with a big bowl of hearty chicken foot soup in our hands—
soup filled with yellow yam, dasheen, coco, pumpkin,
carrots, and cho-cho—
provisions from the heart of the earth,
and dumplings rolled up thick and fat
for the extra fillings.
And with each spoonful brought to our mouth,
the aroma of fresh seasonings released—
with the twirling, rising steam.

Sunday Mawning Breakfast

Sunday mawning,
Sunday mawning—
breakfast was hefty,
hefty and healthy.
Johnny cakes and steamed callaloo,
ackee and saltfish, and roasted breadfruit,
liver with boiled green bananas—
that was an option too.
Fried eggs and bread wouldn't do.
Sunday mawning,
Sunday mawning—
breakfast was hefty and healthy,
kept us going until
Sunday dinna, ready.

Fresh Sunday Juices

A refreshing memory of Sunday
quenches my spirit.
Juices of pine, carrot, and soursop—
one or the other
was a big jug of freshness every Sunday.
Grandma's mood dictated whether it's blend
with condensed milk, nutmeg, a little dash of vanilla...
Or if she felt like it,
sugar and lime was always right.
Oh Lord,
if only I could just have one more glass.

Easter and Good Friday

Holy, holy, holy—
Easter and Good Friday.
Days set aside fi escovitch fish,
and Easter bun and cheese—
holy hardo bread too
was blessed unto us.
Everyone felt the rhythm of the atmosphere.
 Silence was the sound of the market.
Quiet was the sound in Allman Town.
Holy, holy, holy—
Easter and Good Friday.
Everybody takes a rest and eats
escovitch fish with hardo bread,
and Easter bun with cheese.

Could It Have Been Our Ancestors Singing Us Lullabies

On rainy days,
it always seem to thunder—
cook-up saltfish with okra, yellow yam,
dumplings, and boil green bananas.
And when lightning claps and the rain sings,
could that have been our ancestors
singing us lullabies
to soothe our restless souls?
And was the raindrops on the zinc roof
their melodies vibrating through,
lulling us calmly and clearly?
"Good old soul food
is our gift to you.
So gift it to the next generation
who a come after yuh,
so dem too can experience
comforting delight—
whether it rains
or whether the sun shines."
Were the lyrics heard.

SIDES & SOUL FOOD

The small things that carry big flavour

Tek Mi Home

Tek mi home.
Tek mi home to
where the coconut palm tree grows,
and where it sways and dances
when the warm breeze blows.
Tek mi home.
Tek mi home to
where the days are hot but not humid,
and coconut jelly wata is given
to keep me hydrated
and quench my thirsty soul.
Tek mi home.
Please—tek mi home.

Tastee Patties Jingle

If I was asked to write a jingle about patties,
I would write it just like this:
When I was a yout' living in the City,
Tastee patties were nice and beefy.
Lips and tongue and mout' bun-up,
'cause Tastee patties were hot and spicy.
Shirts and dresses get soil and messy,
'cause Tastee patties were flaky and juicy.
If you tried one, yuh will nyam two,
'cause Tastee patties were yummy, fi true.

Plantain

Green or ripen,
boiled, roasted, or fried—
breakfast, lunch, or dinner—
it is nice anytime.
Served with all your favourite dishes,
and sometimes just plantain alone would do.
Buy it by the bunch:
 half dozen,
one dozen,
single or two.
Plantain in every household,
rich or poor.
Ask yuh granny
and her next-door neighbour, Miss Sue—
they will tell you this is true.

Solomon Grundy

Solomon Gundy,
gwan wit' yuh hot peppery smoked herring self.
You are your best self
when yuh spread out pon Excelsior crackers
like margarine and best butta.
Gundy—some called you pâté,
but me called you unforgettable tasty.
I wonder if you are still on the island, curing?
And if you continue bringing pleasure to the palate
receiving you.

Roasted Breadfruit

Dis is a cultural offering:
breadfruit roasting outside
on an open coal fayah,
while Grandmodda inside the kitchen,
cooking ackee and saltfish fi dinna—
and children lurking,
with dem mout' watering,
waiting for the serving.
Roasted breadfruit served with the national dish—
ackee and saltfish adds an authentic cultural twist.
Bring us back a yaard,
 for dis is an unforgettable cultural offering.

DESSERT:
SWEET ENDINGS

*Sweet reflections, joy, play and cultural
cravings to close the feast*

May to June is Peak

May to June is the peak.
I used to see dem dangling from the
trees–
the fruits of the season
East Indian and Julie,
Blackey and Hairy,
Number 7, and number 11,
Green Skin and Green Gauge,
Graham and Stringy,
Fine Skin and Keith,
Cow Foot and Millie,
Hamilton and Kidney,
Robin and Bluie,
Bambay and Beefy,
Emperor and Perry,
Bellyful and Longy–
Sweetie Come Brush Me.

Pick them off from the tree,
Or pick dem up from underneath.

Buy a half-dozen or more
from the lady at market,
or buy a bag or three
from the man pon di street.

Nyam dem green and salty,
nyam dem ripe and juicy.
Yes, mi dear–

mango season is here.

StarFruit

Starfruit, Starfruit—
a jimbilin, bright yellow with a tinge of green,
and your soury, tangy flavour
are what I remember.

Sweetness

Psssst!
Hello dear!
A how you sweet so?
You look like suga extracted from yuh—
brown and white, fine and coarse—
a you got all of us asking for more and more.
Wah gwaan,
tall and slender sweetness?
Yes, you tropical sweet thing—
standing upright and erect,
showing us how proud you are.
You reside where sun not shy to smile,
and the rain pours with joy.
So yes, show off your confidence,
'cause a you got the saccharum sweetness.
And even when we take a bite
and chew through you,
we could never spit your delightfulness
into the gutter of wastefulness.
Cause you are the sugar cane—
the sweetness that none of us can resist.

Tamarind

Encased in brown armour,
but unprotected from the teeth
of the devourers,
we cracked into it
and untangled the string-up, string-up
entrapments within,
and released this soft,
delightful splendour of sweet-tanginess.
Just consuming it wasn't enough.
We had to roll tamarind into balls of treats,
sprinkled with white, sparkling, sugary decor.
And when we desired more from tamarind,
we stewed it in the gingery, sugary pot
of caramelization.

Stew June Plum

I remember all so well
the days of the last bell
of the school day.

Happy and eager I was
to run to Miss Gloria's stall–
I think that was her name.
Mi can't rememba fully,
but I can recall there is always a "Miss" in
front of the names of the elderlies.

My memory recalled undoubtedly:
the stewed June plums tied in plastic bags,
submerged in caramelized ginger, brown sugar, and
cinnamon,
and kept warm by the heated sun.

They were always soft and juicy–
even the prickle seed mi chewed up.

Stewed June plums.
They were an after-school treat
that remains present in fi mi memory.

NaseBerry

Nase-berry,
neese-berry—
brown and fuzzy.
Nase-berry,
neese-berry—
sweet and juicy.
Naseberry,
neese-berry—
small and plumpy.
Nase-berry,
neese-berry—
firm
in my memories.

How to Eat A Guinep

I always savoured di taste–
one by one.

Peeled the green skin with my teeth–
dis is the part I do not eat.

Twirled and twirled di edible portion
inside my mouth,
rolled it, rolled it over mi tongue.

Mi suck,
mi suck,
and mi suck
till all the guinep jelly part
swallowed down.

Mi chewed up the seed–
I never spit it out.

Yes, mi dear,
mi also swallowed dat down.

Fruitarian Pickney

Let me share the days with you—
the days when mi gathered
fallen almond fruits.
Fruits that didn't fall far from its tree,
red with patches of yellow—
they were closer to an orangey colour to me.
Bruised, but yet plump to eat,
I sat beside dem and gathered them,
one by one, and piled them beside me.
I was an unknowing fruitarian pickney.
Mi wiped them down clean with my hands,
and ate until the seeds became naked—
skinless and fruitless.
With a rockstone, mi broke them in half,
until the almonds were free to be eaten.

Allow My Licks Of Love To Melt You

Creamy, delectable you—
I rather they coned you into scoops of two.
Allow my licks of love to melt you
slowly, but before the island's sun captures you.
Unlike Johnny Osbourne,
I wanted ice-cream love—
two scoops of grape-nuts
or rum and raisins.
Or both would do.

Everyting Coconut

Everyting coconut.
Jamaicans irie, mon—
so everyting coconut.
Sunday's rice and peas, dem naah leave out dat—
everyting coconut.
Rastaman's ital food—
everyting coconut.
Sweet gizzadas and drops—
everyting coconut.
Mackerel rundown, all dat—
everyting coconut.
Stew peas, mi haffi mention dat—
everyting coconut.
Toto and grater cakes—
everyting coconut.
Bustamante sweetie, mi dear—
everyting coconut.

Coconut Drops

I cannot remember when I first tasted it,
but I will never forget how it tasted.
Dis brown, irregular-sized confection—
brown like my complexion—
with brown sugar and spices,
and coconut dices.
Drops—an unforgettable taste,
dat is one of the Jamaican niceness.

Sweeties

My memories reminded me
of the days when Lanaman's sweetie factory
was just down the road pon Arnold Road,
in Allman Town, Kingston 4.

And once upon a time,
the scent of all sorts of confectionery
fumed the Town,
and children were playfully happy all around.

Gluttony for paradise plum and Bustamante sweeties
was a sinless act,
because children did no wrong
where sweeties were involved.

The sweet and sourish paradise plum
left evidence of red and yellow paint on our tongues,
and Bustamante, with bursts of coconut and molasses,
stuck to our gums.

Mint balls and icy mint freshen inside our mouths,
And ju-ju left sugary residue outside on our faces,
where evidence of consumption were easily found.

And if Piñata was one of our childhood games,
we would have hit that horse with all our might and strength,
and watch:

toffees, ginger logs, car sweeties, peanut brittle,
cigarette-shaped sweeties, lollipops, bubble gum,
mint balls, icy mint, paradise plums, and Bustamantes–
all of dem fall and shower us like raindrops.

And all the adults would've let us be free,
with a lifetime of sweeties to eat.

A Note To Chippies

Dear Chippies,
mi know you from a long time ago.
In my childhoodness,
I knew no others but you.
Green bananas were your forte.
I had no interest
whether you were fried or baked.
You were salty, crunchy, and tasty—
   just how I loved you.
I travelled to foreign land and carried you
in the palm of my heart.
And so I had compared you with others.
But as the saying goes—yuh live and yuh learn.
Because there is no comparison.
Oh Chippies, I will never let you go stale.
You will always remain
a fresh staple in the unforgettable part of my life.
Yours sincerely,
Chippies Banana Chips Lover

Childhood Memories

Childhood memories—
tek mi back home to sweet sweet
food and families.

It Nicer When It Soft and Warm

There is something about ginger, nutmeg, and cinnamon—
something about dem when dem
  mixed and blend up with vanilla, brown sugar, and flour.
And I have no doubt other things are
  mixed and blend up with dem too.
And so, with all this mixing and blending,
created something that me love—
from when me was a young, young pickney gal
a grow up.
And I know you must be thinking:
what is this something?
This something that is mixed and blend up
with vanilla, flour, and brown sugar.
I know I got you thinking.
I got you thinking
that this something must be truly nice
with all its spices.
So mi must reveal—
bulla cake, when it is soft and warm,
it is truly one of Jamaica's nicest.

Food of Thoughts

A reflection and
recalling of the past,
 of childhood memories.
I know now that food
is a family connector,
a friendship binder,
a cultural language.
It chat Jamaican tongue
loud and proud.
Food is the world discoverer,
a lover and laughter maker,
a conversation instigator.
It is a celebration of life.
Food is poetry.
Food is a story.
It is a storytella.
It tells the stories of yesterday,
today and tomorrow.
Food is truly a nurturah and a heala.

Di Land of My Birth

Dis likkle island is di land of my birth.
Mi navel string buried deh,
deep under its rich, rich soil—
yes, deep beneath the ground,
where June plum and mango trees' roots spread out,
connecting to the roots of mi family tree.
The tree that sprouted
from the West African uprooted seeds,
replanted in Westmoreland, Hanover, and Kingston City.
Jamaica, Jamaica—the land we love,
out of many one people echoes throughout.
So smile for me, Jamaica—yuh a deh the land mi love.
Come mek me and yuh wheel and tun to mento.
Come mek me and yuh skank to ska.
Come mek me and yuh rocksteady to the rhythm
and beat of roots rock reggae.
Haul and pull up, wheel an' come again—
di dancehall selecta a tek we pon the river, pon di bank, once
again.
So come—
come mek me and yuh hold each other tight, tight, tight,
and whine up, whine up we waistline.
Come nuh mon,
come mek me and yuh dance close till the sunrise.
Oh island in the sun,
where the saltwater breeze mix and blend up
with the sweet, sweet pimento seed.

Lawd—the jerk pork and jerk chicken
mek the island wind sweet, eeh!
Jesus Lawd—escovitch fish and bammy
 is a nice piece a tasty treat
 when yuh a sit by the sea.
Ackee and saltfish deh—
island national dish,
serve with roasted breadfruit.
When yuh nyam a plate a dis,
it mek yuh hum and sing.
Whoe—look how mi mout a run wata
when mi memba, memba mi Grandma Wawa:
sweet, delicious coleslaw,
brown stew chicken,
and rice and peas.
Yes fi real, Jamaica—
yuh peoples' national tongue
full a rhythm, full a lyrics,
full a deh beat a we ancestor's love.
Miss Lou honour it inna Jamaica Labrish.
Mutabaruka, Lillian Allen—celebrate it inna dub poetry.
No ma, no sah—nuh weh nuh betta dan yard.
Mi seh, no ma, no sah—nuh weh nuh betta dan yard.
Yes Jamaica,
 yuh likkle—
 yuh likkle but yuh tallawah.

Tradition is Tradition

And so it was—
all the hustling and bustling,
and the excitements.
Rememba.
Rememba
all the painting and decorating.
Rememba.
Rememba the
frilly-frilly new sheets
and new brand bed spread pon di bed.
Rememba.
Rememba the
new tablecloths—red and green ones—
colours matched the
new curtains, lacy and long.
Rememba.
Rememba what we hear down the road—
the same sound from the same church bell.
Rememba.
Rememba
we tek a stroll
inna
new shoes, new dress,
new pants, new shirt.
Rememba.
But when we drink the sorrel,
and eat the black cake,

and the rice and peas,
brown stew chicken,
curry goat,
oxtail...
Rememba.
Rememba—
the taste remain the same.
Wasn't new—
it was the same welcoming, authentic taste
year after year.
Rememba—
tradition is tradition.
Hope we never forget dem.

For Notes & Sweet Memories